THE
ALPHA ASIAN
MINDSET

By James Chan

THE ALPHA ASIAN MINDSET

By James Chan

Published 2009

About the Author

James Chan has been faking adulthood for 21 years. To support his Alpha Asian lifestyle, James works as a police detective for the University of California Police Department. He is also a contributing writer for Planet Muscle Magazine and has authored a series of popular bodybuilding books, titled "Strength and Physique."

To read more of his musings on the Alpha Asian lifestyle visit his blog at:

http://alpha-asian.blogspot.com

TABLE OF CONTENTS

I: What's an Alpha Asian?

I run a blog titled **Alpha Asian**. Sometimes I get a reader that asks, "Alpha Asian? What's that mean?"

And I respond, "Means I'm one badass motherfucker."

An Alpha Asian is someone who lives his life based on self-determination and duty to his community. Being Alpha has a negative connotation in modern society. We often picture someone who is Alpha as a dumb jock who's a control freak. He's often pictured as the Type-A asshole that takes charge of every situation and orders everyone around.

Being an Alpha Asian, however, is not about being the typical overbearing Alpha male archetype, but having a confident and positive frame of mind. An Alpha Asian is someone who lives his life on his terms. You can be a nerd or a jock, but as long as you do what you want to do and do it with style and confidence, then you're an Alpha Asian. Being an Alpha Asian means being the best version of you.

Most people, however, have a *colonized mindset*. They live their lives without ever fully tapping into their potential, and thus without ever being truly happy. Asians are notorious for being mentally colonized. We're incredibly bright and talented people, but we hardly ever fulfill our potential due to the restraints we put on ourselves.

Back in college I majored in psychology, and since then I've always been fascinated by how people self-actualize and tap into their full potential. On the flip side, I wondered why so many people who are clearly talented or smart NEVER fully tap into their potential. Fact is there are very few self-actualized people running around. Most of us are the proverbial icebergs with only the tip of our potential showing above water.

Most people are mentally colonized: unfulfilled potential due to lack of confidence, lack of emotional development and lack of experience. Most Asian Americans tend to be mentally colonized, because our ancestral cultures have made us particularly vulnerable to the mentally detrimental effects of assimilation, racism and bigotry. Our ancestral cultures stress self-effacement, humility, modesty and conformity, and yet we as Asian Americans live a cultural environment that detests all of these qualities.

As Asians, we hold ourselves back more than anyone, and because we hold ourselves back, we're never truly happy. Despite the fact that we as a whole we are intelligent, driven and talented, we are the most disrespected, under-acknowledged and under-confident people in the world. We are overqualified and underpaid both figuratively and literally.

Don't Wait for a Savior: Be A Role Model

Once I was talking to a fellow Asian American about Asian American issues, and he said, "If only there was a leader among Asian Americans, somebody we can rally around."

Let me tell you: if you wait for a savior, he or she may never come, and you would have wasted your entire life saying, "If only..."

Most people, regardless of color or culture, tend to be followers. Not everyone is meant to be a leader, and that's OK. After all, it can be kind of lonely being a leader, not to mention stressful trying to help everybody who's looking to you for answers. Not everyone in our community can be a leader, but everybody can be a role model. Just be a damn good expert at something people have an interest in, and people will respect you as an individual and look past skin color or eye shape.

Let's take Bruce Lee, for example. If one were to think of an Asian guy who was a true alpha male, Bruce Lee would come out first on everyone's minds. The guy was tough and powerful, had a rock hard physique designed to kill and he was extremely articulate, thought-provoking and charismatic. He inspires people of all ethnicities to this very day. People didn't see him as "that Chinese guy." They referred to him by first name, "Bruce." He was so good at what he did and so passionate about his art, that people didn't look at his race but acknowledged how meaningful his work was.

The fact is you can't change other people's perception of Asian Americans, but you can be a role model in whatever it is that you have a talent in and a passion for, whether you're a cop, an actor, a teacher, a musician or a doctor. How people perceive you is how you perceive yourself. People acknowledge talent and they acknowledge expertise. So be the best at something. Be so good at something that people look beyond your race.

This book is a collection of my writings from the Alpha Asian blog with some new material. I talk about everything from psychology to Asian American culture to attracting the opposite sex. In these writings I talk about how to live your life on your terms, while mitigating risk.

It's been 35 years since Bruce's death. Don't wait another 35 years for the next Bruce Lee to save the Asian American community. Be a role model. Do something you love, and do it well.

II: Cultural Dissonance is Ruining Your Life

"Learning too soon our limitations, we never learn our powers."
~Mignon McLaughlin, *The Neurotic's Notebook*, 1960

In our society, the ideal male is confident, eloquent, outgoing and a leader of men. Confucian societies, however, just don't encourage individual expression as much. Humbleness, selflessness and humility are values that are stressed more. Your good work and good character should be evident to others. Although these are admirable qualities, Westerners tend to interpret them as weakness and asexuality.

It wasn't always like this in Asia. After all, you can't run a country when everybody's a follower and nobody's a leader. In ancient, ancient times (and I mean ancient!), there were a lot of wars in China. Kingdoms would fight for supremacy. Stronger kingdoms would swallow up weaker kingdoms. Barbarians would invade. Times were tough: plenty of famines, plenty of poverty and plenty of war.

So when Confucius developed his writings on personal and governmental morality and social relationships, he wrote it with the idea to bring peace and harmony to a region of the world that was in constant chaos and anarchy. When the Chinese people read his writings, they thought, "This is powerful stuff! This will bring peace and order to China. We can all get along."

The powers ruling China thought, "This IS powerful stuff. Who needs an army when we can control a population of millions through these writings... but let's do some major editing first."

So the Confucian writings were rewritten, and an ideology that would empower the people would now enslave them. As a result, social and political relationships became rigidly hierarchical and complete obedience to superiors was emphasized. The "Mandate of Heaven," which states that the people have the right to overthrow a tyrannical leader, was conveniently left out.

Thousands of years passed, cementing this Neo-Confucian cultural ideology throughout much of Asia. So while nice humble guys are valued in Asia, nice guys are considered BORING here in the States, a country built on revolution and independence (not to mention the genocide and enslavement of people of color).

The Immigrant Mentality

Tough times make tough people, however, which is why there are Chinese communities on every continent with the exception of Antarctica. An immigrant by definition is not passive, but a risk taker. After all, it takes a lot of balls to go on a quest for riches in a foreign and hostile land when you don't even know the language.

Yet the Chinese and other Asians are viewed as passive, submissive and adverse to risk. Why is there such a big fat disconnect between perception and reality?

Most of the Chinese immigrants of the Diaspora come from the Guangdong region. Historically this region of China has a long tradition of seafaring, and because the region has always been so far from the capital and from government rule, the people of this region have been coming and going for hundreds of years despite periodic government restrictions on immigration.

Before Confucianism took hold in China, the Cantonese as a whole were a fiercely independent, individualistic and outspoken people. There's a reason why the martial arts revenge movie genre originated in Hong Kong: you can't rely on the government to mete out justice. Justice is personal and something that you take an active role in to ensure its outcome. And it feels good to kick someone's ass for being a dickhead.

Confucianism, however, stresses hierarchy, duty, modesty and assimilation. So when the ideology took over in the region, a duality of culture was created.

The Cantonese and other peoples of the Guangdong region immigrated to other lands, and they tried to assimilate somewhat to avoid being a target. This is why American Born Chinese (ABC) tend to take on Western names. At the same time, the Cantonese tried to keep their cultural heritage intact but subdued and hidden. This is why the middle names of ABC's are their Chinese names.

This Confucian need to assimilate, however, is compounded in American society. Asian Americans care so much about what others think of them, that it makes them susceptible to an exaggerated form of assimilation where they pander to whites and crap on their Asian brothers and sisters.

In order to assimilate, you don't rock the boat. You don't fight the system, because your parents taught you subconsciously that back in the old country, fighting the system gets you killed. You are already racially marked as an Asian, so standing out or raising a ruckus over your troubles just gets you into trouble.

In a sense ABC's are more passive than Asian immigrants, because they were raised to be this way. They were not taught how to articulate their anger over injustices, because their parents weren't able to articulate it in English themselves.

As an ABC, once you realize this dual aspect of your Chinese American culture, things become much clearer. You learn that you have a unique cultural blend that has many strengths but with a few weaknesses that need to be addressed. To be a true Alpha Asian, you learn not to care so much about what others think, and instead you care about real consequences.

Historical Lessons from the Japanese American Community

Asians tend to over assimilate, since their ancestral cultures emphasize conformity, but of all the Asian ethnic groups in the United States, Japanese Americans have assimilated the most. They have the greatest percentage of out marriage of all the Asian American ethnic groups, and this is true for both men and women. Japanese Americans have married primarily white and Chinese Americans.

There are a number of reasons why the Japanese American (JA) community is disappearing. Although the JA community has been in the US for over a hundred years, it hasn't had a constant influx of immigrants, like the Chinese American or Filipino American communities. As a result, most Japanese Americans are third, fourth and fifth generation.

A big factor in the assimilation of the JA community was World War II and the internment camps. Being marked as an enemy based on your eye shape had profound effects on the psyches of many Japanese Americans that have lasted generations later.

Prior to World War II, there was a huge Japanese American community on the West Coast. The relocation had removed this community, and when the war was over, the JA community dissipated across the United States. Very few returned to the West Coast.

In an effort to mitigate post-war animosity that would result when Japanese Americans were reintroduced back into mainstream society, the War Relocation Authority told the JA community three things:

1) Don't go back to the West Coast to live.

2) Don't cluster together.
3) Assimilate as much as possible and don't call attention to your Japanese heritage.

The trauma of internment had stripped the JA community of cultural pride and knowledge. When you don't have a proud cultural heritage to give you strength and perspective, then you're more prone to being influenced by the greater society, who may not have your needs in mind.

Although the Japanese American experience is an example of institutional racism stripping a community of its ethnic heritage, other Asian American communities experience a constant assault on their cultural pride. This erosion of cultural pride can lead to negative consequences, most notably a lack of confidence and esteem. Without confidence and esteem, then happiness can never be truly fulfilled.

Unlearn What You Have Learned

Asian Americans have to unlearn the thousands of years of cultural baggage that they have inherited. Not all, but a lot of Asian Americans need to unlearn their self-effacing demeanors. Not only this, but we also need to overcome the deleterious effects of a white supremacist ideology that has been woven tightly into American cultural fabric.

The bright side is, most Asian Americans grow out of the internal colonized mindset and develop confidence, initiative and leadership abilities after college and when they start working in "the real world." When you work and have to deal with people of different backgrounds to accomplish a goal, then you learn to be resilient. Some of that cultural baggage starts to unravel just enough so that you're confident and relaxed but not an overbearing asshole.

III: Mental Colonialism

"It's hard to fight an enemy who has outposts in your head."
~Sally Kempton, *Esquire*, 1970

The Difference Between Cats and Dogs

Do you know what the difference is between cats and dogs? While both animals behave in accordance with their instincts, a dog accommodates to its master, whereas an owner accommodates to its cat. A cat carries herself as if she were descended from a great heritage: lions and tigers. A cat knows his proud and regal lineage, and let's you know it too.

A dog is also descended from a great and noble ancestry: wolves. But whereas a cat remembers her heritage, a dog does not. Hence because of this cultural amnesia, he's vulnerable to having his behavior molded to fit the needs and wants of people.

So what are **you**? Are you a cat or are you a dog?

The Kubler-Ross Model Applied to Asian Americans

Everybody knows of the Kubler-Ross model on grief, but not everybody realizes that this is the name attributed to this theory. The Kubler-Ross model states that when one must deal with a tragedy or a loss, the person undergoes 5 stages:

1) Denial
2) Anger
3) Bargaining
4) Depression
5) Acceptance

The funny thing is you can apply this model to Asian American psychology. In a sense, the Asian American experience (at least in the old days) involves loss: many Asian Americans feel culturally disinherited, whether it be a disconnect from the ancestral culture or marginalization in Western society.

The Asian American in Denial- This person strongly denies his/her Asian heritage and is extremely whitewashed. S/he feels a sense of superiority to other "unenlightened" Asians who aren't as assimilated as him/her. In his/her mind, the white way is the right way. Unfortunately, college education has made this person an arrogant, condescending asshole.

The Angry Asian Man, a.k.a. Bitter Asian Man- This guy (it's almost always a guy) feels the entire world is out to get him. He is an injustice collector and constantly gripes about how the world is doing the Asian man wrong. He is passive-aggressive and will bitch about a wrongdoing long after the incident has passed. Don't get this guy going about Asian women and white men, or he'll get crazy on your ass.

The Bargaining Asian American, a.k.a. The Yellow Uncle Tom- This guy/gal panders to white people all the time. He is the Chinese waiter who will greet white customers with the warmest smile and treat you like shit. The comedian Esther Ku is a prime example of the Asian who thinks, "If I trash my own kind enough, white people will like me... they'll really like me!"

Usually, this strategy backfires, because nobody likes a traitor.

The Depressed Asian American, a.k.a. the Internally Colonized- This guy is constantly whining about how his Asian heritage is a liability in some way: "I'm too short, because I'm Asian," "Girls won't date me, because I'm Asian," "The media stereotypes Asian people."

Blah-blah-blah. Bullshit, bullshit, bullshit. The depressed Asian American is depressing, because his mind has been colonized to think, "I'm a victim, because I'm Asian," and "White media/society/people are all-powerful," so "I can't do anything, so what's the point?"

This guy needs a kick in the ass and good shot of self-esteem.

The Asian American Who Accepts Him/Herself- This Asian American accepts himself for what he is, but is always to looking to enrich his life with experiences and develop as a person. He doesn't constantly refer to his Asian heritage, unless the situation requires it. He understands that he is an Asian American, but as an individual, he is much more than that. He will defend Asian Americans interests, because he believes in doing what is right for all people.

The Angry Asian Man Syndrome

My friend (who happens to be an ABC like me) and I were talking a couple of nights ago about how Korean men seem rather uptight and angry all the time. He told me, "Yeah Korean women are so beautiful and nice, but the men are just assholes."

Of course, my friend was generalizing. But then again, maybe the Korean guys were trying to cock block him.

I've known plenty of Korean men, and they weren't hot-headed gun-toting whack jobs. Koreans are damn hip, actually. Most of the Asian American celebs these days are Korean: Yul Kwon, Daniel Dae Kim, Bobby Lee, John Cho, Sung Kang, etc. There does, however, seem to be a rash of "angry Asian men" nowadays, not all of them Korean.

The angry Asian man syndrome is also known as "running amok":

"Although commonly used in a colloquial and less-violent sense, the phrase is particularly associated with a specific sociopathic culture-bound syndrome in Malaysian culture. In a typical case of running amok, a male who has shown no previous sign of anger or any inclination to violence will acquire a weapon and, in a sudden frenzy, will attempt to kill or seriously injure anyone he encounters. Amok episodes of this kind normally end with the attacker being killed by bystanders, or committing suicide."

Yeah, not exactly the right way to make people feel comfortable, I have to say.

Anger, like any emotion, is either beneficial or detrimental, depending on how and when it's expressed. Acute anger is good ONLY if it is an appropriate response to a grave injustice. Acute anger is an immediate response, and because the response is immediate, the offender learns not to cross your path again. Acute anger has nothing to do with the severity of your response, but the swiftness of it.

But chronic anger is different. Chronic anger is not expressed immediately and reasonably, so it festers and debilitates the person who is angry. Passive-aggressive people suffer from chronic anger. Injustice collectors suffer from chronic anger.

Chronic anger is indicative of someone who is (or perceives himself to be) in a weak or low status position. After all, if you take offense to every perceived slight, then you must have a fragile ego.

If you're an angry Asian man constantly bitching about how all Asian women are supposedly dating white guys, then that indicates low status and low self-esteem. It is indicates that you're a loser, because you *think* that you're a loser and now you've perpetuated this self-fulfilling prophecy.

So for all the angry Asian men out there: chill out and relax a bit. I know it's hokey, but read up on the Law of Attraction. Better yet, have lots of safe sex. You won't be so angry, and you'll be much mellower.

"Nothing reduces the odds against you like ignoring them."
~Robert Brault

Mental Colonialism

It's one thing to acknowledge racial stereotypes and negative perceptions, but let's not give these perceptions any more influence and "truth." Stereotypes are quite powerful, and sometimes these stereotypes are used as tools to keep groups of people down. Not only do stereotypes affect the perceiver ("I think Asian males are unattractive"), but they also affect the person encapsulated by the negative perception ("I'm unattractive, because

I'm Asian").

Stereotypes are powerful, because you don't need a standing army to police a group of people. The people will police themselves.

If you bitch a being a loser, then you ARE a loser. You can't fight an enemy that's colonized your mind. You have to let go of limiting beliefs, such as racial stereotypes imposed on you by others. Acknowledge them, but quit psychoanalyzing that shit and focus on actions and game plans that will get you what you want.

Jet Li once said something similar and very Buddhist: "I can't change other people. I can only change myself."

Bottom line: Buck the stereotypes. Don't let yourself be dictated by them. True activism for a community means fully actualizing its people.

IV: The Alpha Asian Mindset

"Whether you think you can or think you can't - you are right."
~Henry Ford

Can You Eat Bitterness?

I love watching reality game shows. There are some really crazy shows with some crazy premises ("Hole in the Wall" comes to mind), but most have one thing in common: how much punishment can you endure for a prolonged period of time?

As a whole, Asian Americans have done very well in reality game shows. The most famous is Survivor winner Yul Kwon, but there are other prominent Asian American Survivors, such as Yau-Man Chan from "Survivor Fiji," the most beloved competitor from the series:

"An atypical Survivor contestant, he achieved much success through his knowledge and utilization of basic physics. This was evident from the first episode. After the repeated efforts of much more muscular contestants, he was the only one able to open a box of supplies the tribe received.

"While others had used various brute force methods to open the box, Chan simply dropped it on its corner onto a rock, opening it immediately. In this way he was also able to beat younger, fitter and theoretically stronger players in challenges. While not shown on the series, he was also instrumental to the creation of fire using spectacles (something not normally possible with concave lenses)."

So why have Asian Americans performed so well in these games of mental and physical endurance and torture? Part of the reason has to do with how Asians deal with suffering. Asians tend to tolerate suffering more and endure it longer. You don't bitch about yourself and your suffering. You don't whine about could've, should've, would've. You just deal with it and move on. You eat bitterness.

This is a good thing if your suffering leads to a desired goal, but not good if people take advantage of you and you don't punish them for it.

But with proper focus on the right kind of suffering (the kind that leads to reward), eating bitterness can be a good thing. If you want something bad enough, then you have to do a lot of hard work and deal with a lot of heartache to get what you want. So ask yourself:

Do you have what it takes to get what you want? Can you eat bitterness?

The Western Will to Dominate

I was watching a movie called "Blindsight." It's a documentary about how a group of mountain climbers from the West help a group of blind Tibetan kids reach the summit of a mountain just near Mount Everest. Blind people are considered cursed in Tibetan culture. Tibetans feel that the blind are paying for sins from a previous life.

There was a line in the movie that stood out. About halfway into the expedition, the crew is having a debate about whether or not to go forward and guide these kids all the way to the top. The head of the school for these blind kids is very protective and says that if they don't reach the top, it's OK.

One of the mountain climbers responds (and keep in mind, I'm paraphrasing here),

"This is the difference between Westerners and Easterners. Westerners always want to be on top. The sherpas never reached the top of Everest, nor did they have a desire to reach the top, until Westerners came."

I hate to say this, but there's a lot of truth to this observation. When Westerners compete or battle, they strive for utter and total dominance. It's a very short-term way of thinking, but they look to completely decimate their enemy, obstacle or opponent. Westerners want to come out on top, and that means their enemies have to lose and lose big.

Asians tend to strategize in terms of: how can I win this battle or complete this task with the right game plan and minimal risk? Westerners value all-out effort. Easterners value maximal efficiency, minimal effort.

There are major exceptions. The first emperor of China, **Qin Shi Huang**, was a megalomaniac of phenomenal proportions. You don't get to the top and unify China without totally annihilating your enemies. You might be familiar with some of his work: the Great Wall of China and the Terra Cotta Warriors.

Genghis Khan was another exception. He always offered a choice to his enemies: complete surrender or complete destruction. If you didn't surrender, then the Mongols would not only kill everyone, but they would salt the earth to the point that nothing lived in the area for generations.

Bruce Lee was an ultra-perfectionist who was ultra-competitive. He had to be the absolute best at everything he competed in. Bruce and actor Van Williams often arm-wrestled on the set of "The Green Hornet," but because he had longer levers (arms), Van always won. This infuriated Bruce at length, so much to the point that Bruce took up all forms of grip training to beat Van as well increase his punching power.

But for the most part, Asians do not seek total victory, control or hegemony.

If they did, then the Chinese would have colonized the rest of Asia and America back in 1421 AD.

I think there is something to be valued in the Western mindset to be the best, although I can do without the condescension, racism and imperialism. After all, how can you know your full potential and contribute if you don't test your upper limits from time to time? You have to aim high and take risks if you want to get ahead.

Life Lessons at 39

Yes, I'm hitting 39. I know people always gripe about getting older. I always hate it when some douche says, "Oh I can't believe I'm 30. I FEEL SO OLD."

You know why people hate getting older? Aside from the fact that your skin starts to sag and your hair starts to gray, getting older reminds you that you have a limited amount of time on this Earth and that you may want to get crackin' on whatever goals you have in life. Every birthday is like a nagging mom that asks,

"So you're X years old now... what the hell have you accomplished so far?"

I guess this is why I like time travel stories. I like sci-fi in general, but time travel stories are my favorite genre within the genre. Something about altering the course of history has always appealed to me:

"Hey James? Hi I'm you from the future. Just a heads up buddy: Look both ways when you cross the street tomorrow. Get a job at a company called Google, dude. Trust me. Oh, and be sure to delete your voicemail messages before your girlfriend comes home."

Alas, I don't have a time machine, but at least I can give you younger Alpha Asians a heads up on what's in store for ya. Here are a few bits of advice based on my humble life experience:

1) Hunker down by the time you hit 30. After college and in your 20's is when you can do whatever it is you want to do, because you have few commitments. If you haven't started a family yet, then the 20's are when you should do whatever it is you want to do to get it out of your system.

You want to backpack around the world? You want to start a business? You want to write a book? Shoot a movie? Be an actor or singer? Then do it.

But by 30 years of age, if you haven't made a living out of your passion, then it's time to get a stable career. No regrets.

2) College first? College later? It doesn't matter. Did you ever look at your boss and think to yourself, "How in the world is this nimrod my boss?"

Well guess what? Unless you got a degree in a specialized field that's in demand, your degree doesn't mean much this day and age. You should get a degree, no doubt. You can't get through the front door without one. But a degree simply means that you're not an idiot. It doesn't mean you're special. Your experience (both life experience and work experience) is what showcases your special qualities.

You can get your college degree early and over with, or you can get it later while you're working. It doesn't matter. We all end up in relatively the same leg of the race anyway.

3) Date around. Then settle down. I'm not telling you to be a whore, but when you're young, you should really meet lots of members of the opposite sex that you find attractive. Get it out of your system before you meet that special someone. People take this all or none approach to everything, including relationships. They think, "Oh this relationship didn't lead to marriage, so it was a failure."

But if you had a great time when you were with her, then the experience served its purpose. Not everything is meant to last, but everything can be a valuable and fun experience.

Young at Heart, Mature in Mind

I've been faking adulthood for 20 years. Seriously, I can't believe some of the adult stuff that I'm doing right now: owning a house, having a career, marrying my beautiful and loving wife, attending department meetings, etc. Sometimes I'm sitting in those meetings in the office, and I think to myself, "Damn, these old guys want MY opinion? Don't they know I *just* graduated college 16 years ago?"

The best way to be happy and wise is to be young at heart, mature in mind. This means you got to have a childlike attitude, where you're flexible, full of imagination and creativity. But you've also got to develop the skills of your mind. To do this, you have to accumulate more varied experiences, to develop your talents and your mental resiliency.

Dream like a child, focus like an adult. Some people have it the other way around: they've got the mental skills of a high school freshman who hates school, but the attitude of a crotchety 74 year old man sitting on his porch with a shotgun.

On the other hand, there are a couple of guys that I work with who seem to be in a state of arrested emotional development. They have a passion for simple things in life: food, strong coffee and good conversation with friendly company. They constantly long for the 1980's.

Yet they seem rather happy despite their lack of planning. One guy lives in a studio apartment in a shady part of town with hardly anything saved up in his bank account, but he doesn't seem to care. He lives his life outside, in the hustle and bustle. He has coffee and lunch with friends, he loves many women and he plans a trip or 2 every year. He sees and experiences the world, everywhere from Mongolia, Japan and the Philippines to London and Amsterdam.

Times are tough right now, no doubt. If you're in-between jobs, however, then see it as an opportunity to get in touch with your inner child and to develop your mind. When I graduated college, it was in the middle of a horrible recession. I had no job prospects and a lot of time on my hands.

So what did I do? I developed myself. I went to the library and devoured a book every week on every topic that interested me. I started working out for the first time and became so engrossed with bodybuilding, that I read everything I could about diet and training. I started writing, fiction and non-fiction. I taught myself HTML to start a website. I traveled and went to Hong Kong and China to see my grandparents for the first time, and I got a better sense of my family history.

All things that happen in life are opportunities to develop yourself, but so are all things that YOU make happen. Be young at heart, mature in mind.

Time's Not Up

Every person in his or her late 20's always laments that when 30 is around the corner your dreams will supposedly end. But for me, things really didn't start happening for me until I was in my thirties. Everything that I wanted to happen started happening within the last ten years. In your 30's, your career is solid, your finances are solid, you've found the love of your life and as result you start a family around this time period. Plus you've got disposable income to buy all the things you want and to travel.

In your 20's you may have some lofty goals, but frankly at that age you don't know jack shit about the world. That's why in your 20's it's about acquiring life experiences. Good times with friends, meeting new people, trying new things. Whereas your 20's are about experiences, your 30's are about accomplishments. That's why everybody who turns 30 looks back and asks,

"What did I accomplish?"

I remember that in my 20's, I had a friend who always had some crazy scheme he wanted me to join him on. Long before Match.com or E-Harmony came on the scene, he launched a dating site when the Internet was still in its infancy. He always wanted to start a business. He always talked about creating a short film and using that film as a springboard to jump into the film industry.

The funny thing is he was always looking for me to be a "partner" in these projects that he came up with, because it was too risky and too much work for him to handle alone. In a sense, he wanted me to be his assistant to help him achieve his dreams.

The problem is you can't wait for other people to start a project. If you do, then you will never achieve anything, because you're using someone else as a crutch or as an excuse as to why you're not making progress. You got to have some emotional resiliency where you say,

"I don't care what other people say. I'm going to do this, and I'll figure out how to do it along the way."

Don't rely on your family, friends or even your spouse or partner to be supportive. You have to rely on yourself. Don't get me wrong. Your loved ones want the best for you, but they want you to get there by avoiding risk.

But for you to be truly successful in whatever you do, you got to focus on the goal, not the risks.

I don't do a lot of rock climbing, but one time I went through a ropes course with a lot of climbing obstacles. There was one physical challenge where you had to climb to the top of a telephone pole, stand straight up on the top of this pole, then jump off and grab a trapeze suspended approximately 5-6 feet away. You would either successfully grabbed the trapeze and floated down to the ground or you would miss the bar and fall 30 feet to the ground (on belay, of course).

I successfully completed the course, because I operated on this game plan: don't look down and focus on your end goal (reaching the top). I never looked down, because if I did, then I would've gotten vertigo and fallen off or been paralyzed with fear (which happened to one guy). I always kept an eye on the top, because that was where I had to be.

A key to success is to gradually expand your goals and build on each success that you have. When I decided to be a writer in my spare time, success to me in the beginning was just completing an article and getting it on the Internet. Then eventually it was to get paid for an article. Then it was to publish a book. Then it was to market the book and actually money from my passion.

I achieved all of the above many times over. It's given me a nice side income, a little extra cash every month for trips and nice dinners with the wife. Each time I published an article, I leveraged it for a greater opportunity. Editors of high traffic sites noticed my articles on low traffic sites and contacted me to write for them. Then I leveraged my online articles to become a writer for print magazines that pay well.

So remember:

1) Build on your success
2) Focus on the goal, not the obstacles
3) Don't rely on others to jumpstart your dreams. Just go out there and do it.
4) You always have time, but you have to start now.

Be Effective and Popularity Will Come

I've never been one to follow convention. I like doing things my way, and I don't give a crap on whether or not it's normal or if I'm doing it the way it's supposed to be done. All I care about is:

1) Do I like doing it?
2) Is it effective and productive?

When it comes to blogging or any other endeavor you undertake, if you are effective, then the popularity will come. People recognize talent, and they recognize B.S. If you are dishonest with yourself, then your readers will smell it.

Most bloggers try to define success by the number of readers they have. They stress quantity over quality. But it is much better to redefine success by the *quality* of readers as opposed to quantity. Who cares if you have 100,000 readers a day if most of them never care to visit your blog again? If that's the case, then what you said obviously didn't make an impression on them.

The key to writing a successful blog is to write for an audience of one, namely YOU. If you write for yourself, then others who are like you will find you. It is better to have a small cult following than for you to follow the fickle masses of the Internet.

I don't write about conventional Asian American issues, because everybody else in the AA blogosphere writes about that stuff. How many times do we have to read about interracial dating and white guys banging Asian chicks? For an Asian American blogger, that's an easy kill, because AF/WM is such an incendiary topic. I don't mind writing about it, but only if I'm adding something new to the discussion that hasn't been said before.

As a blogger you have to respect your audience, and that means you don't dumb things down for them. You have to hold your audience to a higher standard. Talk to your audience as if they've already done their homework and know certain basic things. If you do this, then you will attract a higher quality of readership. In essence, you will influence the influencers.

When I write the Alpha Asian blog, I write not with the intent to be popular, but to be effective in bringing more hope, confidence and charisma to the Asian American presence on the Net.

Alpha Asian Code of Conduct

Asian Americans have a unique psychology that is a result of their transcultural upbringing. We've learned to infuse the best aspects of both Western culture and Asian culture to discard the emotional baggage from both cultures. If you want to think and act like an Alpha Asian, then operate with these principles:

1) Avoid passive-aggressive behavior. I hate to say this, but Asians tend to be very passive-aggressive. Culturally, we've learned not to be directly confrontational, because a direct confrontation with someone of higher status, power or authority could have painful and even deadly repercussions.

But in Western society, passive-aggressive behavior is seen as weak and untrustworthy. Although you see a lot of passive-agressive backstabbing behavior in American reality shows like "Big Brother." In general, however, passive-aggressiveness shows that you were too slow and too timid to respond to transgressions with enough strength and quickness. Be direct when you can, and avoid passive-aggressive behavior.

2) You MUST defend yourself and your kind. In "The Apprentice," Donald Trump would always fire the guy or gal who didn't speak up for him or herself in the boardroom.

Trump's reasoning is "Why the hell should I hire someone to defend my interests, if this person cannot even defend himself?"

When you or your family or friends are attacked, you must defend yourself. If you do not defend yourself, your loved ones or your ethnic group, then no one respects you, your loved ones or your ethnic group. Why should they respect you if you don't even respect yourself?

Asians and non-Asians have very different responses to being bullied. Here's a scenario that's been played out at a playground or two: If an Asian boy were bullied at school by a non-Asian boy, then the Asian kid tends to shut down and not respond. He tends not to give any verbal or bodily cues that he's going to defend himself.

In his mind he's thinking, "I'm not giving you any trouble, so back off."

In response, the non-Asian kid sees the lack of defensive cues as weak and proceeds to pick on him some more. Even though the anger is escalating within the Asian kid, he does not show any signs of this anger until the very last minute. By then the Asian kid goes all out and starts pummeling the other, who is caught completely by surprise. Afterwards, the two shake hands and become friends.

Sound familiar? Nip bad behavior in the bud and defend yourself immediately.

3) Actions speak louder than words. Americans and certain European groups tend to talk a lot about what they supposedly are, what they've supposedly done and what they supposedly will do. Asians see such behavior as bragging and consider it arrogant. For Asians, actions speak louder than words. Who we are should be fucking apparent.

Humans are hardwired to detect deception, because detection of deception is vital to survival. Nobody gives a fuck what you say you are or what you say you've done. Did you do what you were supposed to do or not? People are constantly comparing your actions with your words, and if the two don't match, then everyone knows that you're full of shit.

So don't be a barking Chihuahua. Do. Don't just talk.

4) Don't devalue yourself. Asians are notorious for being Uncle Toms. They have this awful habit of putting themselves down or putting other Asians down. I cannot stand people who constantly refer to their ethnicity or somebody else's ethnicity. If someone mentions my race and there's no justifiable context for mentioning it, then it means this person is uncomfortable with me being Asian, so much so that he or she mentions it without any prompting.

If you're Asian and you refer to your Asian heritage without any conversational reference, then YOU have a problem with your ethnicity. Non-Asians crack enough jokes about Asians already. So don't encourage that shit by cracking racist self-deprecating jokes in front of them.

Practice these principles daily and don't get discouraged if you can't follow them a 100% of the time. Just focus on success and build on it when you can.

<u>10 Op Orders for the Alpha Asian</u>

These are some of the life lessons I try to live by. It took me years to figure some of this stuff out:

1) Be honest with yourself. It's one thing to be dishonest with others, but nobody respects a person who is dishonest with himself. Know what it is you ultimately want. Don't bullshit yourself and say you want one thing, when you really want another. Be very objective in your self-analysis.

2) Learn to focus, and focus on the right things. You may have a lot of lofty and grandiose dreams and ideas, but if you can't focus on doing the daily tasks that help accomplish those dreams, then you are of no use. Learn to focus on a few activities, and do those activities well. Just make sure that whatever activities you are engaging in are meaningful and will result in measurable and desirable outcomes.

3) No regrets, no guilt. I don't ever feel guilty. You know why? I don't act stupid in the first place. If you feel guilty, then it means you were too stupid to refrain from performing the regretful act. Guilt helps no one after the fact.

4) Minimize the negative, maximize the positive. The Chinese metaphor for life is war. This means life is always lived strategically and tactically, and to do this, you must always minimize the negative and maximize the positive.

5) Commit to your goal, not your methods. Life is a series of battles, however, and each battle is situational. Learn when your strength can become a liability and when your weakness can be transmuted into strength. Go with the flow. What is important is your goal, not your methods.

6) When you commit, commit totally. When you make a choice and commit to a course of action, perform the action with confidence. Commit fully, and you will succeed. Hesitate, and you will fail.

7) Reward well, punish swiftly. Avoid passive-aggressive behavior. Nobody respects a person who stews over an incident, but did not have the confidence to address the perpetrator the moment it happened.

8) Always prepare. Always be prepared. Don't allow yourself and your loved ones to be placed in bad situations. Take ownership and avoid bad situations in the first place. Win every battle before it is fought.

9) Be information dense, word sparse. Words carry more weight, when one speaks less. If you want to get your point across, then be direct. If you want to listen, then be vague.

10) Do what you like. Be happy, stupid! Why make yourself miserable? What good are you if you're the human equivalent of Eeyore? Don't wallow in self-pity. Act. Do what you like.

Four More Op Orders for the Asian American Activist

1) Don't look for a leader. Be one. If you develop yourself and accomplish things, then share your expertise with the community. Improving the Asian American community is best done from bottom up, not top down.

Most people think that change comes around when the government intervenes or when a non-profit organization goes on a campaign to improve the community. It's a very top-down mentality that is very condescending: "We lead. You follow."

It is much better when idea viruses spread, and individuals change on the inside. How the hell is someone going to help and contribute to the community if he or she doesn't have their sh!t down in their personal lives? If you give people the tools and the psychology to enrich themselves, then the community is better as a whole.

2) Create instead of react. If you look around the Asian American blogosphere and the Asian American forums, most people are reactionary. Most people use the Internet to vent and rant about how non-Asians are racist. Fact is most non-Asians are prejudiced against Asians. Nothing that whites, Blacks or Hispanics surprises me anymore. I assume they're doing the chinky-eye behind my back every chance they get... those racist bastards!

A paraphrased quote from Harvey Milk puts things in perspective, "If I turned around every time someone called me a faggot, then I'd be walking backwards. And I don't want to go through life walking backwards."

3) Don't ask for respect. Earn it. Asians tend to be Confucian-conformists, so they constantly worry about what others think: "Gee, what do white people think about Asians?"

Who gives a crap? Seriously, if your esteem and happiness are based on what others think, then you might as well get some therapy.

4) Pure academics insulates from real world experience. Asians stress academics, and that's great. But real world experience is what counts. I've known plenty of people who had to work through school, and they ended up ahead in life because of their time dealing with people and managing a business.

A professor of mine at UC Davis did a survey of all the famous geniuses in history and his findings revealed this: revolutionary geniuses (really smart and innovative people who change the world) don't stay in school past the 4-year degree. Geniuses with rigid thinking (you know, the boring ones who join Mensa) get graduate degrees. These geniuses maintain the status quo, whether or not it is ideal.

Bottom line: Do, don't just talk.

The Biggest Distractors

Distractions: everybody has distractions in their lives that keep them from achieving their goals. Some "distractions" really aren't distractions but obligations, such as family and career: "Damn it, woman! If it wasn't for you and the kids, I'd be a famous writer by now!"

But some things are just a big fat waste of time. I'm guilty of all three of these:

1) TV- I used to watch lots of TV, but now I can't stand to watch any more than 2 hours a day. It has to serve a purpose for me to watch it, which is why I watch History Channel documentaries a lot. I do watch comedy standup to decompress, and reality shows to observe human behavior. "I Survived a Japanese Game Show" is one I've been watching lately. Bottom line is not to watch TV during the day, because it will just chew up your time. Watch it in the evening when you want to relax.

2) The Internet- I think Internet addiction is a real phenomenon. Prior to a weekend trip, my wife jokingly asked if I needed to bring the laptop. Checking your email, surfing the net and blogging take up quite a bit of time, and it feels like you're getting stuff done. But in reality, the Web is just chock full of distractions. I just don't get social networking sites. Great way to find people, but boy, is that a waste of time. If you want to keep in touch with me, then just send me an email. The Internet can be a great resource where you can write books, create sites and voice your opinion, but you can also waste a lot of time with frivolous stuff.

3) Books- This might surprise you, but sometimes books are big distracters for nerds. Unless you write fiction in some form (movie/TV script, graphic novel, etc.), fiction books are some of the biggest distracters for sappy nerds. Who wants to read about life? Go out and live it. Women tend to fall in this trap and form book clubs (even more distraction). I used to read a lot of sci-fi as a kid, but now I read a lot of nonfiction books on topics that further my interests: health, marketing, psychology, Internet trends, bodybuilding and strength training. But there is only so much reading you can do. You have to go out there and apply your research. I think people who read too much use research preparation to stall and procrastinate. What helps me is to practice a little bit of speed-reading and go through books at a faster rate. Take what's useful and move on.

The 3-5 Method

I love the board game "Risk." Risk is a classic board game about world domination. You teach yourself a lot about strategy and managing your resources. If I were to pick 4 classic board games to teach your child to develop a mindset that can deal with the real world, it'd be:

1) Risk (for strategy and tactics)
2) Monopoly (for resource and financial management)
3) Scrabble (for vocabulary)
4) Chess (for mental calculations)

Anyway, there's an episode of Seinfeld where Newman and Kramer are playing a days long game of Risk, and Jerry comments,

"It's Risk. It's a game of world domination being played by two guys who can barely run their own lives."

Some people are like Kramer: a lot of crazy ideas that border on genius, but they got A.D.D. You know the ones I'm talking about. They'll go into a diatribe about the history of Chinese oppression in Tibet or preach against whale fishing by the Japanese, but they can't manage a checkbook or lay off the booze and weed. They don't have their shit together in their lives, so they choose to rally around causes on the other side of the world so they can swing their moral hammer.

I've talked a lot about focus in my previous blog entries, and focus comes in handy when it comes to choosing causes and pet projects to fight for. As some of you know, I train and write about strength training and bodybuilding in my spare time.

Bodybuilders know how to focus, because they are mindful of the moment they are in. People who don't like hardship will bitch and complain about an exercise being too painful and will stop the set prematurely. But a bodybuilder is totally focused on that burning sensation in his muscles. He embraces it thinking, "I LOVE working through this pain, because I know it will get me to my goal."

A bodybuilder focuses on the hard work in the gym that gets shit done. Here's a bodybuilding method that I've adapted to prioritize pet causes and the effective actions to be undertaken. It's called the 3-5 Method.

The premise is simple: keep lists of any kind to 3-5 bullet points, NO MORE. Anything beyond 3-5 is not relevant. Develop 2 lists: one list of 3-5 goals you **want** to accomplish no matter how long it takes, and one list of 3-5 goals that can easily be accomplished right away.

If you have a severe case of A.D.D. and more poor time management skills, then do 2 lists of 3. If you're focused and driven, then do 2 lists of 5.

The great thing about this method is that if you get bored with one project, then you can rotate to another project on your list that you're in the mood for. That way you can recharge, but not be pulled in 10 different directions.

V: Career Philosophy for the Alpha Asian

"If you really put a small value upon yourself, rest assured that the world will not raise your price." ~Author Unknown

Are you happy with your job? I don't know if it's the crowd I hang out with, but I have never met anybody who was truly happy with their job. Everybody from doctors to high paid consultants to computer programmers and cashiers and admin assistants: everyone wanted to do something else with their lives. You would figure that the more you're paid or the greater your status, you'd be happier, but it's just not the case.

People get the method or means mixed up with the goal. They think if they're promoted or had a better job, then they'd be making more money and have a higher status, and that this would lead to happiness. But it's really the other way around: if you're happy, then opportunities open up for you. It's easier to be happy than it is to change your situation. I know it sounds ridiculous, but being happy is about reworking your mindset:

Do you want what you have?

If you don't want what you have, then can you alter it to make it what you want?

Two great books on this very topic are "The 4 Hour Work Week" and "Refuse to Choose." These books both agree on one thing: your time is more valuable than money. With a fixed amount of money, you can only buy so much. But with time, you can do whatever you want. You can make money, you can spend time with family and friends, you can tend to your hobbies or you can lie in bed and watch the paint peel on your ceiling. With time, it's up to you.

Everybody grew up with this lie, that when we finished college we would have a high paying job doing what we loved. We feel as if it's our birthright.

But the fact of the matter is that most people aren't doing what they're passionate about. Their jobs aren't exactly horrible, and some jobs pay well. But people get depressed when they realize what they're doing as a job isn't the same as what they love doing.

Well I say, "Who cares?!" That's what the weekends are for.

The key to happiness is to do what you like whenever you can. It just doesn't have to be your job. If your job is your passion, then congratulations: you've attained what 99% of us will never attain. But as long as you have time to do what you like, to be with people who you love, then that's what counts.

This brings me to the other key to happiness: people. They can make you happy or they can make you miserable. Your boss and coworkers all affect your happiness with your job. If you have a demanding boss, then he or she can make your life a living hell. But you may love your job and your coworkers.

The keys to happiness are to do what you like even if you're not being paid for it and to spend time with your loved ones: friends and family.

I've been at my current job for 10 years. That's very rare in this day and age, especially amongst my generation (X) and after. I've never met anybody whose job was truly his or her passion. I've never met anybody who was truly happy with his or her job to stay longer than a few years.

With some exceptions, everybody I've known has always moved around from job to job. I was like this too in my 20's. I once quit a job on the very first day. At one point, I was working 3 part-time jobs at the same time. There wasn't a full-time job out there that I liked, so I created a composite with 3 part-time jobs I did like.

Of course those of us who have jobs should be happy these days. Nevertheless, some of you may feel distraught being trapped in a job you don't like. Here's some tips on how to maintain career longevity:

1) Underpromise, overdeliver- Don't promise the world and fail to deliver. If you do that repeatedly, then everybody knows you're full of sh!t. It's much better to provide your boss or your customers *reasonable* expectations as to what will happen. Then do a damn good job. This way you'll exceed expectations and look like a miracle worker.

2) Good work gets you more work- If you do good work, then you'll get more work because everybody knows you get stuff done and done right. This is either good or bad, depending on your work environment. If you run a business, then doing good work gets you more business. More business means more money.

If you work in the public sector, then good work gets you more work, but you still earn the same pay as the lazy bum watching YouTube the next cubicle over. This doesn't mean you should do bad work (since that gets you fired), but learn to say no to work that somebody else is supposed to be doing.

3) Shear sheep, don't skin them- If you manage and supervise people, then keep this saying in mind when you hand out work. You might have a star player on your team, and you'll think of him as the go-to guy or think of her as the go-to gal for everything. Be careful, however, because if you overwork your star player, but don't compensate him with higher pay or extra perks, then he's going to have a mental breakdown and leave for another position with a company or department that will properly compensate him.

4) Be a specialist, not the go-to guy - If you don't want to promote, because promoting to a higher position means longer hours and more responsibility, then be a specialist in something that your company needs. Police departments, for example, have lots of specialty assignments, such as detectives, defense tactics instructors, K9's, etc.

VI: Attraction and the Alpha Asian

"Sex appeal is fifty percent what you've got and fifty percent what people think you've got." ~Sophia Loren

I recently had lunch with a friend, and she related how she had broken up with her boyfriend. She's a very intelligent girl and like anybody fresh from a break-up, she feels confused and somewhat betrayed. The reasons for the break-up didn't seem logical to her.

The thing is that intelligence, logic and rationality have NOTHING to do with attraction and maintaining relationships. Both men and women do stupid things when they are possessed by emotions such as passion, sexual tension and longing. There is a widely quoted phrase among PUA circles and that is this:

"Attraction is not a choice."

You can't help whom you're attracted to and when you're attracted to someone, no matter how intelligently and rationally you behave and live your life. This is the reason why some women are attracted to bad boys or make bad choices with regards to their love life. This is why a man risks everything he's earned, including his marriage and his financial assets, to have an affair.

A perfect example of this is to ask an "open-minded," "liberal" woman if she would date or marry a short guy, and she will tell you, "No." Attraction to height is hard-wired into our genes and there is no getting around that. Another example would be to ask an "open-minded" male if he would date someone ugly, and he'll tell you "No" as well.

I took a lot of Asian American Studies courses, so I knew a lot of Asian American professors. With the exception of one couple, every Asian American professor I knew (male and female) that was attached was married to a Caucasian spouse. We're not talking about professors who masquerade as Asian American Studies professors and teach Amy Tan. We're talking about people who contributed to seminal Asian American works, like "The Big Aiiieeee!" We're talking about hardcore fighters for the Asian American community.

You would figure proponents for Asian American respect would have married Asian American spouses, but like I said: attraction is not a choice. To deny that you feel attraction towards someone, even if it is based on bias and irrationality, is stupid. Acknowledge your desires, acknowledge your biases, because we all have them.

Attraction Switches

I think what it comes down to is that women are very complex creatures (my wife is the queen of complexity) and that they prefer men with a mix of masculine and feminine characteristics. A woman needs to know that the guy she's with is able to protect and provide for her, but also has some sensitivity, some part she can emotionally bond with and that her children can bond with. Some women do prefer big "beefy" men, but they only make up 10-20% of the population.

Not only that, but women can be fickle. They kind of have to be, because it's a huge investment for them emotionally and physically (child birth) and they can't be with someone who is one extreme (ultra-masculine, super macho bad boy) or the other (extra sensitive and super boring nice guy). There was a recent study that indicated that women were more attracted to bad boy types as they got closer to their period. But most of the month, they preferred nice stable guys. I think a lot of it has to do with a woman's rise of circulating hormones toward the end of the month.

Women tend to be more complex and ever changing in their preference for men. Dr. Drew Pinsky puts it bluntly:

"Men have one attraction switch. You turn it on. You turn it off. Women, on the other hand, have a cockpit full of attraction switches. Each woman has a different cockpit with a different assortment of switches."

This is by no means an exhaustive list of attraction switches, but these are the most common:

1) Sense of Humor- It's cliché, but by far the most quoted trait women are looking for in a man is a sense of humor. Why would a sense of humor be important in attraction? Well, a woman has to be comfortable with you and open to revealing feelings to you. She doesn't feel comfortable with you if you're a serious, stern fuddy-duddy talking about boring subjects. A woman has to be entertained to some degree, but she also wants to know that you have a positive outlook on life that she can share in.

2) Leadership/Social Status- Women go for men who are leaders in some capacity. If you can lead other men, then you can certainly provide for her and protect her and her children.

3) Articulate- This is closely related to number 1 and 2. If you are articulate, then it shows higher status. Chances are you have a higher education, and this is appealing to women. Communication skills are important, because this is how you relate to other people and develop a greater social network. The greater your social influence, the better you are at providing for your partner.

4) Hobbies/Interests- In order to be interesting to a woman, then you have to have interests. When you have interests, it shows that you have depth. Women want to connect with someone who has some kind of depth and complexity. Otherwise you're just boring.

5) Looks- There's no denying that looks play an important part in attraction. But *why* are looks so important? The things both men and women value in appearance (clear skin, nice hair, hourglass figure, etc.) are indicators of health. When women are checking out a guy physique, they tend to look at height, broadness of shoulders and the butt (yes, the butt!). The funny thing is that their tastes depending on what time of the month. Women prefer more masculine facial features when they are ovulating, and less masculine features the further away they are from ovulation.

6) Provider- This is a no-brainer. If you've got a high status/high-paying job, then women will overlook your looks to a large degree. This may paint women as cold and mercenary, but if you look at it from a woman's perspective, then it's completely understandable. Why invest your time and emotions with someone who has no aspirations?

7) Sexuality- This may seem obvious, but if you don't exude sexuality and don't convey yourself as a sexual being, then no woman is going to think of you that way. Don't be a walking dildo, of course, but flirt on a regular basis. If you don't flirt, then you lose that skill. Then you're a eunuch, figuratively speaking.

The trick is to turn on as many of these attraction switches as you can. My wife put it to me simply, "I don't ask for much in a man. I just want him to have it all."

VII: The Alpha Asian Diet

I think we've all noticed this effect when we travel abroad, whether it be Asia or Europe: we lose weight! It's interesting to note that many countries eat far more carbohydrates than Americans (notably China and Italy), and yet people from these countries weigh far less than Americans. Much of this has to do with the fact that people in other countries tend to eat smaller portions, and they walk or bicycle everywhere. Plus, Americans react very poorly to stress, which increases the amount of abdominal fat on your body.

Since Asian countries have become more Westernized and affluent, however, their diets have included more meat and more fats. The Okinawans are the most long-lived people in the world, but unfortunately, younger generations of Okinawans are encountering health problems due to the consumption of fast food.

In China, there is a phenomenon called the "little emperor syndrome," where due to the one-child policy "both parents lavish attention and resources on their one child, the child becomes increasingly spoiled and gains a sense of self importance and entitlement." (Wikipedia)

An effect of this syndrome has been overweight boys. The parents send these boys to physical education classes, much the same way as one here attends a cardio class or yoga class.

A culture's cuisine not only affects body composition, but the cultural psychology as well. Koreans eat lots of seafood, meat, veggies and spicy food, and they're stereotyped as hotheaded. Many Indians are vegetarians, and as a result India produced Gandhi, Buddha and yoga. Coincidence?!

Or how about the Mongols: meat and dairy, very little carbs. And they lived the Old World's equivalent to the Hell's Angels lifestyle.

The effect of diet on psychology is quite profound. Consider the brainwashing techniques of the Russians. You would figure that starvation would break a person down and make his mind malleable, but it has the opposite effect: one becomes more focused. If you feed someone nothing but carbohydrates (no protein, no fat), then you fuck up his serotonin levels. Serotonin is a neurotransmitter that modulates anger, aggression, mood and sleep.

When it comes to my favorite cuisines for a healthy lean body, I'm very partial to the Asian cuisines. Asians tend to live longer than other racial groups partly, because of their diets. Asian cuisines tend to have less meat and more veggies and fruits than Western cuisines.

Ever since I've read the book, "The China Study," I've experimented with lowering my animal protein intake and upping my vegetables. If you haven't read the book, what it essentially says is that the lower your intake of animal proteins, the lower your risk for cancer, heart disease, diabetes and a whole slew of other diseases. It provided some very compelling evidence, compelling enough for me to reevaluate some of my assumptions concerning vegetarianism. In descending order, here are my top three healthiest Asian cuisines:

3) Chinese: There are MANY different types of Chinese cuisines, since China is such a vast country with many regions, subcultures and ethnicities. But what makes Chinese cuisine healthy is the high amount of vegetables and tea (green and black). Where non-Chinese botch things up is with the stereotypical dishes they eat: sweet and sour pork, eggrolls, etc.

Daoism influenced Chinese cuisine, where you have a balance of foods that are categorized as either yin or yang. Vegetables are yin: very cooling and calming to your body. Beef, poultry and pork are very yang, causing inflammation in your body.

If you think this is shamanistic mumbo jumbo, then let's break it down scientifically: yin foods (vegetables) create an alkaline state in your body; yang foods (meats) create an acidic state in your body. People who have been diagnosed with cancer are typically placed on a vegetarian diet to alkalize their bodies' pH, because cancer cannot grow in an alkaline environment.

2) Korean: The great thing about Korean food is that it most closely resembles a Paleolithic diet: meat, seafood and vegetables, minimal sweets and starchy carbs. This is the ideal diet for those wanting a lean muscular body that is also healthy on the inside. This is a great warrior diet.

1) Japanese: There are 4 great things about Japanese cuisine: green tea, miso soup, seaweed, and a lot of fish. Each one of these foods will add years to your life. It is no wonder that the Japanese (and more particularly the Okinawans) are the most long-lived people in the world. Where non-Japanese botch things is when they order tempura (a dish Portuguese in origin).

VIII: The Alpha Asian Workout

Let's face it: people respect strength. People respond to you differently when you're built like an ox and have arms that look like they can easily rip a phonebook in half.

Conversely, people tend not to respect skinny guys. I should know: I used to be a stereotypical skinny Asian guy. If you're a skinny Asian dude, then it's tough. You're not sure if people don't respect or take you seriously because you're short, skinny, Asian, young or all of the above.

I didn't realize the impact a muscular physique can make on people until I started working out. When your forearms resemble bundles of steel cables, people subconsciously realize this:

1) You're strong.
2) You've put in some hard work and hard time to become strong.
3) You're disciplined enough to do the hard work and the hard time to become strong.

These qualities earn you some respect, regardless of your background.

As a strength trainer with an Asian American background, I often get questions and comments from Asian dudes all over the world. A common theme that pops up among Asian lifters is the belief that their Asian genes are limiting their progress in their quest for a muscular physique.

I always tell them this: don't let race or ethnicity be a limiting factor in your training goals or any goal. It does not matter if you are Asian or a skinny bastard or a woman. If your goal is to be bigger, faster, stronger, then you still travel the same road that everyone else travels to size and strength.

Plenty of Asian men from a variety of backgrounds have developed some rather impressive muscular physiques:

Bruce Lee

Once during the filming of "Enter the Dragon" the director's wife, Ann Clouse came onto the set and was mesmerized by Bruce's rock hard physique as he was choreographing the fight scenes. Ann approached Bruce and asked if she could "feel his biceps."

Bruce obliged and she gasped, "My God! It's like feeling warm marble!"

If one were to think of an Asian guy who was a true alpha male, Bruce Lee would come out first on everyone's minds. The guy was tough and powerful and had a razor sharp physique designed to kill. He was extremely articulate, thought provoking and charismatic. He inspires people of all ethnicities to this very day. People didn't see him as "that Chinese guy." They referred to him by first name, "Bruce." He was so good at what he did and so passionate about his art, that people didn't look at his race but acknowledged how meaningful his work was.

I remember growing up as a little kid watching his movies and feeling a sense of pride in my Chinese heritage, something I didn't feel prior. What amazed me at the time was that all of my childhood friends and classmates who were white, black and Hispanic all wanted to be Bruce and emulate him. That's the thing with Bruce: he was so extraordinary that people looked beyond his race and recognized the impact of what he brought to the world.

"If you're talking about combat, as it is, well then baby: you'd better train every part of your body!"

- Bruce Lee from "The Lost Interview" 1971

When Bruce took up strength training to supplement his martial arts training, he did so solely for the purpose of increasing what he called "real world power." The phenomenally ripped physique that he had was simply a by-product of all of his martial arts, strength and cardiovascular training.

Bruce experimented with all types of strength conditioning programs, but Bruce was fond of two strategies in particular: isometrics for muscle tone and circuit training for conditioning.

Circuit training is also known as "peripheral heart action" or PHA training. PHA is the exact opposite of the traditional bodybuilding strategy of pumping or flushing a muscle. In circuit training, you strive to circulate blood throughout the entire body rather than localized in one muscle group. You do this by moving from one exercise to another exercise with little or no rest in between. Typically you string together 8-9 exercises in a circuit, alternating between upper and lower body exercises. Go through the circuit 3-5 times, resting a few minutes between circuits.

The advantage of PHA training is that it will increase cardiovascular conditioning and your strength endurance. You will lose a lot of fat while maintaining or even gaining muscle.

Isometrics is when you tense a muscle at a single point in its range of motion. Isometrics quickly develops strength and muscle tone. You can perform isometrics by:

1. **Pressing or pulling against a fixed object** (i.e. pins in a power rack)
2. **Holding a weight stationary for a prolonged period of time**. A perfect example of this was when Bruce would stand, raise a 125 lb barbell in front of him at arm's length, elbows locked and hold that position for several seconds. Quite an amazing feat of strength considering he weighed only 10-20 pounds more than the barbell.
3. **Simply tensing your muscles**. Bruce always wowed audiences when he spread his lats like a cobra. Doing bodybuilding poses like the lat spread is a form of isometrics. Bruce also developed razor sharp abs with an isometric/isotonic exercise known as the "Dragon flag," where he would lie down on a bench and flex his trunk and legs off the bench and over the edge.

Ninja Warrior

Aside from the fact that "Ninja Warrior" is an extreme test of strength, coordination, endurance, skill and agility, what I like about this Japanese TV show is that everybody and anybody can compete, and you don't know necessarily who's going to be successful. You've got Olympic gold medal gymnasts and firefighters competing with gas station attendants and crab fishermen.

Some of these guys get obsessed with the show and build their own obstacle courses in their backyards. Just imagine that you're the wife of one of these dudes and one morning you find your husband out in the back: "Uhh... honey? Why is there a gigantic circular ramp in our yard?"

People from particular athletic backgrounds will do well on the show: gymnasts, Parkour enthusiasts (also known as traceurs), acrobats and mountain climbers. These athletes develop a lot of grip strength as well as general upper body strength, so they are well suited for the rigors of Ninja Warrior, which has a stage devoted solely to upper body strength endurance.

These athletes also have impressive V-tapered physiques: broad shoulders, muscular arms, wide backs and trim waists. This look is appealing to both men and women. Men respect the V-taper for its strength, and women admire it for its sexuality. In many cases these athletes (gymnasts in particular) develop incredible bodies without ever touching a barbell, dumbbell or machine. They rely solely on their bodyweight to train, and the awesome look they have is simply a byproduct of that training.

You may not want to undergo the rigors of Ninja Warrior training, but you can certainly emulate the look of a Ninja Warrior. If so, then train like a gymnast and focus on calisthenics or bodyweight exercises:

1. **Pull-ups and chin-ups**: By far, this is the most important exercise for upper body strength and development. DON'T USE THE MACHINE

ASSISTED PULL-UP, EVEN IF YOU CAN'T DO A PULL-UP. Hang from the bar and work on doing real pull-ups.)

2. **Parallel bar dips:** While the pull-up is the most important exercise for upper body strength and development, dips are a close second. Again, DON'T PERFORM MACHINE ASSISTED DIPS, EVEN IF YOU CAN'T DO A DIP. If you can't do a full-range dip, then support yourself on the parallel bars and perform partial dips. Over time work on increasing the range of motion until you can dip all the way down.

3. **One-legged squats, a.k.a. "Pistols":** These require a lot of practice and flexibility, but once you're able to do them, pistols will leave you quite sore in the quads. To perform pistols, lower yourself on one leg while extending the other leg out in front of you. Sounds easy enough. If you don't concentrate, however, then you'll fall on your ass. Keep these points in mind when performing pistols:

- If you've never done pistols before, then perform half reps over a park bench. Over the course of several workouts, increase the depth of your squat.
- Extend your arms out in front of you to counterbalance your torso as you squat down.
- Round your torso and back over the knee of the leg doing the squatting. By curling your torso over your knee as you squat to the bottom, your center of gravity stays directly over your base, which is your foot. This will help you avoid tipping over.

4. Hanging leg raises:

- With an overhand shoulder width grip grab an overhead bar and hang.

- Tighten your grip and flex your lats and abs.

- Curl your trunk and raise your feet up to the bar, keeping your legs semi-straight.

- Try not to lean back as you raise your legs to the bar. As you raise your legs, try to curl your body in and "crunch" your abs.

- Lower your legs and repeat, keeping excess momentum to a minimum.

Tommy Kono

Outside of the sport Olympic weightlifting, very few people know of Tommy Kono. Among weightlifters, however, Tommy Kono is considered legend and the greatest lifter the U.S. offered to the world. He set world records in four different weight classes, a feat that has been unmatched. He won the gold medal at the 1952 Olympic games in Helsinki, Finland and again at the 1956 Olympics in Melbourne, Australia.

By the time he was inducted to the International Weightlifting Hall of Fame in Switzerland, Tommy Kono established 26 world records and seven Olympic records. Tommy also "dabbled" in bodybuilding and winning the Mr. World physique title once and winning the Mr. Universe three times.

Weightlifting and bodybuilding are two different endeavors. Weightlifting is an athletic event concerned with performance (how much weight can you lift). Bodybuilding is a physique event concerned with aesthetics (who's got the best look of mass, muscularity and cuts). Nevertheless, weightlifting does have carryover to bodybuilding, because you develop a lot of explosive strength. Having this explosive strength provides a solid foundation for you when you lift to gain muscle. Here's Tommy's philosophy on training:

"The U.S. lifters have to go back to the American system of training and not follow what the Europeans are doing. The lifters must return to basics and not have tonnage or intensity govern their training. Believe it or not, it is the old system of light, medium and heavy; training 3 to 4 times a week and each workout lasting no more than 90 minutes. It is a matter of taxing your muscles and giving ample time to recover. Too many of our current lifters are over-trained and getting injuries because they lack the recovery time."

In other words, it's much better to train the entire body briefly and frequently. Don't follow a split routine, and vary the intensity from workout to workout, instead of all out effort all the time.

The Alpha Asian Workout

The following is a weight-training program inspired by Tommy Kono's principles of training briefly, frequently and with varying effort, but with a bodybuilding focus. This program consists primarily of free weight exercises, so it's an ideal workout for home gyms. Many bodybuilders like to use machines, but using machines to get strong is like pedaling a bike with training wheels and claiming you know how to ride a bike.

Be warned: this is an extremely difficult and physically grueling program. The routine is meant to put muscle on an intermediate level bodybuilder. If you stick with the program and get lots of protein, calories, water and rest, then you will gain a tremendous amount of muscle.

This is a two phase program: follow phase one for 2 weeks, then follow phase two for 2-3 weeks.

Density Phase: 2 Weeks

DAY ONE

/ 20° Dumbbell Bench Press (3) 6-8
\ Pushups (3) as many reps as possible, 2:00

/ Lying EZ-curl bar Extension (4) 5-7
\ Lying Dumbbell Extension (4) 5-7, 4:00

/ BB Back Squats (3) 15-20
\ Sissy Squats (3) as many reps as possible, 3:00

Romanian Deadlifts (3) 3:00

DAY TWO

/ Pulldowns (3) 8-10
\ Seated Cable Rows (3) 8-10, 3:00

/ Seated Dumbbell Laterals (4) 10-12
\ Standing Dumbbell Laterals (4) 10-12, 2:00

Biceps Triset
- Zottman curls (3) 6-8
- Incline curls (3) 6-8
- Barbell curls (3) 6-8, 3:00

Dumbbell calf raises (2) 5 drop sets for each leg, 6-10 reps each drop set, 2:00

DAY THREE- off

DAY FOUR

Front Squats (3) 8-10 cluster reps, 2:00

Barbell Bench Press (3) 12-15 cluster reps, 2:00

Dumbbell Rows (3) 8-10, 2:00

Rear Laterals (3) 8-10, 1:30

One Legged Calf Raises- bodyweight only (3) as many reps as possible, 1:00

/ Lying to Seated Curls (3) 10-12
\ Elevated Diamond Pushups (3) as many reps as possible, 1:00

DAY FIVE- off

DAY SIX

Flat Bench Dumbbell Press (3) 6-8, 2:00

Pull-ups (3) as many cluster reps as you can perform, 2:00

Deadlifts (3) 4-6, 2:00

Seated Dumbbell Laterals (3) 20-25 cluster reps, 2:00

Barbell Preacher Curls (3) 8-10 cluster reps, 2:00

Lying Barbell Half Press in power rack (3) 8-10 cluster reps, 2:00

One-legged calf raises (perform 100 total reps with bodyweight only, alternating between legs with no rest)

<u>DAY SEVEN</u>- off

Program Notes for Density Phase:

- "/" and "\" indicates that the 2 exercises are a superset, one exercise performed immediately after the other, followed by rest.
- "( )" indicates the number of sets. Hence "(3) 6-8" indicates 3 sets of 6-8 reps.
- "0:00" indicates length of rest between sets. Hence "1:30" indicates 90 seconds.
- To perform cluster reps, take a given weight where you can only perform half of the required reps. In rest-pause fashion, you will stop rest briefly, resume the set and repeat until you achieve the desired number of reps. For example, if a set of bench presses requires 12-15 cluster reps, then it would look like this:

   - You perform 8 reps
   - You rack the weight and rest for 10 seconds
   - You resume the set and perform 4 more reps
   - You rest for 10 seconds
   - You resume the set and perform 3 more reps for a total of 15 reps

Decompression Phase: 2-3 Weeks

<u>DAY ONE</u>

Back Squats (4) 10-8-6-15, 2:00
20° Barbell Bench Press (4) 10-8-6-15, 2:00
Close Grip Pulldowns (4) 10-8-6-15, 2:00
Swing Laterals (4) 10-8-6-15, 1:30
Dumbbell Calf Raises (4) 10-8-6-15, 1:30

DAY TWO

/ Zottman Curls (4) 5-7, 2:00
\ Lying EZ-curl Bar Extensions (4) 5-7, 2:00
/ Incline Hammer Curls (4) 5-7, 2:00
\ Standing Barbell Overhead Half Press (4) 5-7, 2:00

DAY THREE- off

DAY FOUR

Barbell Hack Squats (4) 10-8-6-15, 2:00
Barbell Bench Press (4) 10-8-6-15, 2:00
Seated Cable Rows (4) 10-8-6-15, 2:00
Rear Laterals (4) 10-8-6-15, 1:30
Dumbbell Calf Raises (4) 10-8-6-15, 1:30

DAY FIVE- off

DAY SIX

Pull-ups (4) as many reps as possible, 2:00
Kettlebell Clean & Press (4) 5-7, 2:00
Deadlifts (4) 4-6, 2:00
Seated laterals (4) 10-8-6-15, 1:30
Dumbbell Calf Raises (4) 10-8-6-15, 1:30

IX: Recommended Books and Courses for the Alpha Asian

Back in college I majored in psychology and minored in Asian American Studies, so I've always had a thing for self-improvement. The key to improving all aspects of your life is improving your mindset and decision-making. Here are some life coaching books for the Alpha Asian:

Awaken the Giant Within- This book by Tony Robbins was the very first self-help book that I ever read, and to this day it still has very profound effects on my mindset. Tony takes neurolinguistic programming to the next level and goes over how you choose your words can shape your beliefs and how beliefs will steer your course of actions. Tony goes over the mechanism of change, and how to use it to make yourself a better person and to make your life better. The great thing about this book is that it goes over SPECIFIC actions to change your mindset, and not vague bullshit philosophy.

The Secret, a.k.a. The Law of Attraction- Do yourself a favor and just rent the DVD "The Secret." This will save you from reading any of the books on "The Law of Attraction." The Law of Attraction is quite simple: what you think of attracts what you get. In psychology, it's widely known that people will mirror each other's emotional states. So if you're a depressing bore, then people interacting with you will display negative emotion and body language. The Law of Attraction takes it further into metaphysics and states that your thoughts will shape the course of the Universe. So if you think shit happens to you all the time, then guess what? It does! If you are more happy and positive, then good things flow your way. This DVD serves as a nice adjunct to "Awaken the Giant Within."

The 80/20 Principle- Mark Twain once said, "Put all your eggs in one basket, AND WATCH THAT BASKET!" The secret to success is be damn good at something people give a shit about. If you can do that, then people will pay you big money for your specialty.

Rich Dad, Poor Dad- All of the "Rich Dad, Poor Dad" books are the same, and frankly, don't give you any concrete advice on how to make money and be rich. What this book does go over is how do you think of money and more generally, what is your learning style? Most of us were taught in school, and school teaches you that failure is not good. But in the real world, failure is how you learn and improve yourself. This is why people who are academically smart aren't necessarily the wealthiest people, and why there are a lot of dumb rich people. Just read any of the books in the series, and the author Robert Kiyosaki will drill it into your head that your money should work for you and not the other way around.

Influencer- Changing yourself is one thing, but how do you influence others for positive change? People always rely on lecture and debate to influence people, but logic and rationality, no matter eloquently laid out, doesn't move people to change. Yet people are taught in school that this should be the primary method of communication and influence. Nobody wants to listen a lecture. Experience is what changes people. Not everybody can go through what you experienced, so vivid and focused story telling is the next best thing.

The 4 Hour Work Week- Rethink your life's course. Why delay your retirement, when you can enjoy mini-retirements through out your life? You may not quit your job and spend a year in Thailand after reading this book, but you will rethink how you're spending your life. The most quoted line from this book: "It is better to beg for forgiveness than to ask for permission."

The Definitive Book of Body Language- I've read quite a few books on body language over the years, but this recent one by Allan Pease is quite good. Not only will you be able to discern the body language of others, but also you'll be cognizant of how you present yourself. Adjusting your body language will adjust your emotional state. So if you want to be confident, then take up a confident body posture.

Refuse to Choose- Do you want to do one thing and do that for the rest of your life? I sure as hell don't, and you shouldn't either. Most people are multi-faceted and have multiple interests. The problem comes when people suffer from "goal paralysis," when they dabble in everything but accomplish nothing. Career coach Barbara Sher goes over how you can pursue multiple interests and live a life of variety and accomplishment.

Essential Asian American Studies Courses

If you're an Asian American college student or if you're not Asian, but you really want to have a better understanding of Asian Americans, then take some courses.

You don't have to major in Asian American Studies. At most, a minor is best. The reason I say this is that it doesn't take that many courses for you to develop an Asian American consciousness. Major in something useful or something that you have overwhelming talent in and passion for. This way you have an understanding of your history, of your community's current needs and of your own psychological-cultural make-up, but you will also have something of value to offer society.

These are some of the courses that I took 18 years ago:

1) Asian American History- History, whether it be Asian American history or ethnic specific history (i.e. Chinese American history), is the foundation of the Asian American Studies program. Without this base, then you won't understand why things are the way they are now for the Asian American communities. Without historical knowledge, then ignorance keeps us in the dark and everyone stumbles over the same issues over and over.

2) AA Literature and Creative Writing- A history course tells a story of a community, but people are moved when stories are personal. This is why news shows do stories focusing on one person. You can have a story about a thousand people dying from a cyclone in India, and viewers will tune that out or not even care. But when a personal experience is told in vivid detail, it is almost as if the viewer or listener were experiencing the events him or herself. Hence, literature and the ability to tell stories is powerful. You can quote several studies and statistics, and it won't mean shit to the common person. Powerful stories, however, move people and get them to empathize or even act.

3) Asians Americans in the Media- I find that Asian Americans fall into 2 categories when it comes to awareness of Asian stereotypes: A) They have no clue about the stereotypes or B) they find offensive stereotypes everywhere, even when there are none.

Taking a course on AA's in Film and the Media is a double edge sword. You can identify stereotypes of AA's, but you'll be seeing these images in everything. If you take a course in AA's in the Media, then don't get caught up in categorizing, analyzing and compiling stereotypes. Because becoming preoccupied with that stuff makes you paranoid, an emotion which doesn't serve anyone. Although I have to say, just because one's paranoid, doesn't mean racist shit doesn't happen.

For a more proactive take on AA's in the media, enroll in an Asian American Film course. With this course you can see how Asian Americans represent themselves in indie and mainstream films and TV.

4) Asian American Psychology and Culture- These courses are not widely available among Asian American Studies programs. To understand and deal with others, you really have to understand and deal with yourself. A lot of Asian Americans want to blame everything on racism and the bigotry of others. The fact of the matter is that racism and prejudice do affect our reality. But the question always comes down to, "Well WTF are you going to do about?"

The ball is always in our court. Racism and prejudice may taint our lives and society, but YOU are still responsible for making things happen in your life. And if you want to make things happen, then you have to understand yourself and your unique Asian AMERICAN culture.

AA culture is a hybrid subculture, no less valid than any other culture. But growing up as an Asian American gives you a unique perspective on things. You have a wider perspective, and hence a better perspective, unlike those who grow up with only one culture.

Unfortunately, since a lot of Asian Americans have grown up in varying degrees of assimilation under Western civilization, there's a lot psychological baggage that has to be overcome. If you're honest with yourself, however, in acknowledging the strengths and problem areas of your ancestral culture and of your personal experience in the US, then you're on your way to becoming culturally whole and self-actualizing.

5) Asian American Women's Studies- Yes, I took this course. No, I did not take it to meet girls. I took it, because I needed to fulfill units for the Asian American Studies minor at the time. I was one out of a handful of guys in that class, which had about 50 students. Nevertheless, it was interesting, because Asian American women have baggage all their own. Thank God, I didn't have to read Amy Tan or Maxine Hong Kingston, because my professor was truly progressive.

I can't say that this is the case for all Asian American Women's Studies courses, because a poorly led course can slowly devolve into a feminist/PC-fascist fest. One time in class, the professor was talking about the fetishization of Asian women, and this one female expressed her surprise over this common fetish and said, "I just went out with a white guy... I could have been raped!"

Develop an Asian American Consciousness and Be Damn Good at Something

When I was in grad school in 1996, I presented at a couple of academic conferences on Asian American Studies: one in Hawaii and the other in D.C. My presentation was titled "Racism and Advertising in 19th America." I had a slide show of all the negative imagery of Chinese Americans in advertising at the time. Very esoteric and very pedantic stuff. My presentation was published as an article in an academic journal, which ModelMinority.com snagged and posted on their site several years later.

Analyzing and cataloging all of those negative stereotypes just burned me out at the time. I didn't feel like I was developing any skills to better the Asian community. My thesis adviser told me something very profound but pragmatic at the same time. She told me, "You want to help the Asian American community? Then get a regular job. Develop some skills and expertise that address the needs of the Asian American community."

When it comes down to it, if you want to help Asian Americans, then develop that Asian American consciousness but also be a valuable asset to the community. A desire to help the Asian American community is great, but you have to offer something substantial that the community can benefit from. Know what your talents are and exercise them to better the lives of Asian Americans and people in general.

Made in the USA
Lexington, KY
31 December 2009